Bible reflections
for older people

The Bible Reading Fellowship
15 The Chambers, Vineyard
Abingdon OX14 3FE
brf.org.uk

The Bible Reading Fellowship (BRF) is a Registered Charity (233280)

ISBN 978 0 85746 619 8
All rights reserved

This edition © The Bible Reading Fellowship 2018
Cover image © Thinkstock

Acknowledgements

Scripture quotations taken from The Holy Bible, New International Version (Anglicised edition) copyright © 1979, 1984, 2011 by Biblica. Used by permission of Hodder & Stoughton Publishers, a Hachette UK company. All rights reserved. 'NIV' is a registered trademark of Biblica. UK trademark number 1448790.

Scripture quotations from The New Revised Standard Version of the Bible, Anglicised edition, copyright © 1989, 1995 by the Division of Christian Education of the National Council of the Churches of Christ in the United States of America. Used by permission. All rights reserved.

Scripture quotations from The Revised Standard Version of the Bible, copyright © 1946, 1952, 1971 by the Division of Christian Education of the National Council of the Churches of Christ in the United States of America. Used by permission. All rights reserved.

Scripture quotations taken from the Holy Bible, English Standard Version, published by HarperCollins Publishers, © 2001 Crossway Bibles, a division of Good News Publishers. Used by permission. All rights reserved.

Scripture quotations taken from the Amplified® Bible (AMPC), Copyright © 1954, 1958, 1962, 1964, 1965, 1987 by The Lockman Foundation. Used by permission. www.Lockman.org.

Poem on page 33 © Andrew Rudd. From *One Cloud Away from the Sky* (Cheshire County Council, 2007). Used with kind permission of the author.

Every effort has been made to trace and contact copyright owners for material used in this resource. We apologise for any inadvertent omissions or errors, and would ask those concerned to contact us so that full acknowledgement can be made in the future.

A catalogue record for this book is available from the British Library

Printed and bound by Zenith Media

Contents

About the writers 4

From the Editor 5

Using these reflections 6

The wisdom of trees Martin and Margot Hodson 7

In remembrance of me Katherine Hedderly 18

The Gift of Years 29

The gift of play Anne Townsend 37

Friends for life Roger Combes 48

About the writers

Martin Hodson is a plant scientist and environmental biologist. He is Operations Director for the John Ray Initiative (JRI), an organisation connecting environment, science and Christianity. **Margot Hodson** is Rector of Wychert Vale Benefice (six churches) in Buckinghamshire, and was previously Chaplain of Jesus College, Oxford. The Hodsons have published widely and have written several books including *A Christian Guide to Environmental Issues* (BRF, 2015). For more about the Hodsons, see their website **www.hodsons.org**.

Katherine Hedderly is Associate Vicar at St Martin-in-the-Fields, London. She has developed the church's work on dementia, bringing together those with lived experience, healthcare practitioners and theologians. Before ordination, she worked in broadcasting for 20 years, including as head of development for an independent production company.

Anne Townsend is a former OMF missionary doctor in Thailand. She is a new contributor to BRF but has written a number of books including *Faith without Pretending* (Hodder, 1990) and was founding editor of *Family* magazine. She is a psychotherapist and a (supposedly) retired priest in the Church of England.

Roger Combes lives in Crawley, West Sussex, with good views of planes taking off from Gatwick. After parish ministry in London, Cambridge and Hastings, he was Archdeacon of Horsham before retiring in 2014. He and his wife Christine have two daughters.

From the Editor

Welcome to this new collection of Bible reflections. We hope you find much to interest and inspire you in these pages, together with some nice surprises along the way.

Last summer, Channel 4 attracted a lot of positive attention for its series *Old People's Home for 4 Year Olds*. Even the most sceptical reviewers were won over by the joyous effects of introducing nursery-school children to care-home residents and allowing friendships to blossom between them over the course of six weeks.

Already popular in the US, Canada and Japan, similar schemes are beginning to take root here too, but you don't always need a formal project to mix the ages so creatively. One of our contributors, Anne Townsend, writes about 'the gift of play', and her experience helping to lead her church's holiday club: 'Three of us "nearly and over-80s" were team leaders. We offered wisdom and experience. Teenage "junior leaders" supported us. Not only were they highly mobile, but their hands could cut and shape in seconds – while arthritic fingers like mine took minutes. It wasn't "Do it my way!", "No, mine's better!" We pooled our resources and played together to build God's church of the future.'

What a hopeful vision of a community in which everyone, from the very young to the very old, has a place and a role, gifts to share and love to give.

God bless you

Using these reflections

Perhaps you have always had a special daily time for reading the Bible and praying. But now, as you grow older, you are finding it more difficult to keep to a regular pattern or find it hard to concentrate. Or maybe you've never done this before. Whatever your situation, these Bible reflections aim to help you take a few moments to read God's word and pray, whenever you are able.

When to read them

You can read these Bible reflections in the morning or last thing at night, or any time during the day. Why not use them as a way of making 'an appointment to be with God'?

There are 40 daily Bible reflections, grouped around four themes. Each one includes some verses from the Bible, a reflection to help you in your own thinking about God and a suggestion for prayer. The reflections aren't dated, so it doesn't matter if you're not able to read them every day. The Bible verses are printed, but if you'd like to read from your own Bible, that's fine too.

How to read them

- **Take time** to quieten yourself, becoming aware of God's presence, asking him to speak to you through the Bible and the reflection.
- **Read** the Bible verses and the reflection:
  - What do you especially like or find helpful in these verses?
  - What might God be saying to you through this reading?
  - Is there something to pray about or thank God for?
- **Pray**. Each reflection includes a prayer suggestion. You might like to pray for yourself or take the opportunity to think about and pray for others.

The wisdom of trees

Martin and Margot Hodson

Do you have memories of particular trees? We can each remember climbing trees as children; as adults, we remember a large copper beech outside our last house; and we now have an apple tree that is especially fruitful. Trees can act as markers through our lives. Often in the background but always giving context, pointing back to the past and forward to the future.

Trees are mentioned hundreds of times in the Bible and in almost every book. Many of these are geographical, helping to show where a story is set, but sometimes trees are used to teach spiritual truths.

These reflections will use the trees as our teachers. We will begin to learn some of the spiritual truths that the Bible's first hearers would have understood, and find out how they apply to our lives today. We will discover how we can be sustained by our roots like the willow and bear fruit like the palm tree even when we stay still and the world changes around us.

So please join us on a spiritual journey through the Bible's woodland and find some truths for your own life from these majestic teachers.

Matthew 17:20 (NIV)

Mustard-seed faith

[Jesus] replied, 'Because you have so little faith. Truly I tell you, if you have faith as small as a mustard seed, you can say to this mountain, "Move from here to there," and it will move. Nothing will be impossible for you.'

The mustard seed appears in two stories in the gospels, one concerning the kingdom of heaven (Matthew 13:31–32) and the other, faith. Botanists have debated which plant species Jesus is referring to in these accounts, as the mustard seed is not that small and its plant is at best a fair-sized shrub (certainly not a tree). But let's put aside the arguments over species and think more generally about seeds and trees. We did a rough calculation and reckon that a mature oak tree is about three million times the weight of an acorn.

The good news is that Jesus clearly tells us that we don't need faith the size of a massive tree, only a small seed's worth. Just a small amount of faith can move mountains. What is it that you need faith for in your life at the moment? It may be a health issue, an upcoming house move or perhaps something you need to talk to a friend about. Remember the mustard seed and have faith.

■ PRAYER

Lord, we know that sometimes our faith can seem very small. Show us how to use that small amount of faith to build your kingdom. Amen

Genesis 8:11a (NIV)

Peace of the olive

When the dove returned to [Noah] in the evening, there in its beak was a freshly plucked olive leaf!

At home, we have an olive-wood holding cross, which is smooth and curved and sits easily in the palm of a hand. It is a reminder of the transforming power of Christ and the connection between his suffering, redemption and healing. The olive is a long-lived tree and highly prized for its fruit. Olive oil is liquid gold as it provides food, light and heat. Priests and kings were anointed with olive oil as they entered service and Jesus' disciples used the oil for healing (Mark 6:13).

The olive tree is first mentioned in the Bible at the end of the flood. Noah sends out a dove and he returns with a sprig of olive, proving the existence of dry land. Because of this story, the olive is a symbol of peace-making and reconciliation. It was no coincidence that Jesus prayed in an olive grove, Gethsemane, as he awaited arrest on his journey to the cross.

Peace can seem an elusive dream for communities and families who long for harmony. The olive reminds us that there is hope. Jesus died and rose again so that one day all things will be reconciled (Colossians 1:20). We can trust Christ's reconciling power working in our world and in our own lives, families and communities.

■ **PRAYER**

Heavenly Father, help us to be bearers of olive branches and bringers of peace. Amen

Isaiah 61:3b (NIV)

Oaks of righteousness

They will be called oaks of righteousness, a planting of the Lord for the display of his splendour.

There is some confusion over the word 'oak' in the Bible. If you look at different translations, sometimes the word 'terebinth' (the tree which produces the pistachio nut) is used and sometimes they cannot decide what species it is and just use the word 'tree'. Whatever the case, these trees were often planted at places of worship and sometimes they were places where loved ones were buried. They symbolised strength, wisdom, longevity and, here, righteousness.

Are we oaks of righteousness? Whatever stage of life we are at, we should all be aiming to live righteous lives. We have been planted where we find ourselves at this time to 'display his splendour'. So we are not living lives that are honouring to God just for ourselves, but because we are God's witnesses to this world. It is not always easy to decide what is the right action to take, but we should definitely avoid things that we know to be wrong. And God will help us with both of these. We just need to ask for his help in prayer.

■ PRAYER

Lord, we pray for people who have been given positions of responsibility. They might be church ministers, leaders of businesses or politicians. We pray that they will lead us in paths of righteousness. Amen

Jeremiah 1:11–12 (NIV)

See the almond tree

The word of the Lord came to me: 'What do you see, Jeremiah?' 'I see the branch of an almond tree,' I replied. The Lord said to me, 'You have seen correctly, for I am watching to see that my word is fulfilled.'

The almond is a beautiful tree. It is the first to flower each year and its Hebrew name means 'hard-working', 'reliable' and 'watching'. Its lovely blossom certainly seems to watch over the Mediterranean landscape as it signals the start of spring.

As the seasons shift in our lives, we can find ourselves to be like almond trees. We are looked to for wisdom and reliability at work, in church and with our families, as younger generations face multiple challenges. Even when retired, there are plenty of opportunities for hard work, with family and community. We also find ourselves watching. There are many good things, for example children succeeding in college and careers, a first grandchild, or even a great-grandchild. There are also difficult things to see: illness and bereavement, marriage breakdown, redundancy or ageing church communities.

God promised Jeremiah that he was watching. When we feel powerless, he is alongside, working in the lives of the people we love and the situations that we care about. He will see his word fulfilled and one day we will see it blossom like an almond tree.

■ PRAYER

Dear Lord, give us strength to be prayerful watchers and give us wisdom to support those we love. Amen

Judges 9:15 (NIV)

Cedar of Lebanon

The thorn-bush said to the trees, 'If you really want to anoint me king over you, come and take refuge in my shade; but if not, then let fire come out of the thorn-bush and consume the cedars of Lebanon!'

Cedars of Lebanon are majestic, long-lived trees native to Lebanon. They appear numerous times in the Bible, but only in the Old Testament. Many times, they are mentioned as being used to build Solomon's temple. Their wood was highly prized as it was strong, aromatic and resistant to attack by insects and decay.

This story in Judges 9 repays reading in full. Abimelek becomes king by killing the 70 sons of Jerub-Baal. Jotham, the youngest son, escapes, and tells a parable to the people of Shechem and Beth Millo in which the trees are all offered the chance to be king over the other trees. One by one, they refuse. Finally, the thorn-bush is made the offer. He sees the cedar of Lebanon as the true king of the trees but threatens that fire could come out of him to consume the much larger tree.

The cedar is the king of the trees, but who is king of your heart? Jesus, like the cedar, is strong, a majestic king and someone you can rely on.

■ **PRAYER**

Lord Jesus, we pray that you will rule over us and we ask for your strength wherever we are now. Amen

Jeremiah 17:7–8a (NIV)

Willow roots

But blessed is the one who trusts in the Lord, whose confidence is in him. They will be like a tree planted by the water that sends out its roots by the stream.

Each year, we teach at a summer school near Berlin for young Christian adults. We stay by a lake and there is a large willow tree right by the water. The willow has its roots deep down into the fertile and well-watered soil of the lakeside. Our students are likewise putting down roots into the Christian faith that will hopefully last a lifetime.

If you had the privilege of becoming a Christian as a young person and have kept an active faith, you will have those deep roots to draw on as you meet new challenges in later life. If you are still relatively new to faith or exploring faith, the good news is that it is never too late to put down roots.

With roots deep in the riverside soil, our willow need not fear, even in a heat wave. It can be devastating when health breaks down or we are shattered by bereavement, but if we nurture our roots, through the habit of daily Bible reading, for example, we can find comfort and peace in the same slow, steady way that roots supply water for the tree.

■ **PRAYER**

Lord, help me to put down roots of faith and to trust you in all the seasons of life. Amen

Genesis 21:33 (NRSV)

To plant a tamarisk

Abraham planted a tamarisk tree in Beer-sheba, and called there on the name of the Lord, the Everlasting God.

Tamarisks are shrubby trees that can reach ten metres in height. They grow mostly in the deserts and wadis, and are very tolerant of drought and salinity. The Bedouin often plant them for shade.

Why did Abraham plant a tamarisk tree at Beer-sheba? Nobody knows for sure, but if you read earlier in chapter 21 it does give some clues. Beer-sheba means 'well of seven' or 'well of the oath'. Abraham came to an agreement with Abimelech over a well and they swore an oath to each other at this spot. It was this that allowed Abraham and his family to remain in Canaan, so it was a very important event. Trees were seen as symbols of life and of blessing by God. On other occasions, Abraham built an altar to honour God, but here it seems he planted a tree.

How do we honour God? We may not build altars or plant trees, but we should all be honouring God in some way. We will honour God by the kind of life that we lead. Whatever our age and whatever our circumstances, we should aim to live lives that will please God.

■ PRAYER

Lord Jesus, show me how I can live a better life, and one that is pleasing to you. Show me how to be a good witness to the Everlasting God. Amen

Psalm 92:12–15 (NIV, abridged)

The fruitful palm

The righteous will flourish like a palm tree… planted in the house of the Lord… They will still bear fruit in old age, they will stay fresh and green, proclaiming, 'The Lord is upright; he is my Rock.'

In the Old City of Jerusalem stands Christ Church, the oldest Anglican church in the Middle East. In the garden grows a palm tree. Its age and fruitfulness point to the fruitful ministry of the church.

Date palms have been cultivated for at least 9,000 years. They probably originated in what is now Iraq and were a familiar fruit throughout the Bible. In Israel, their branches are cut for the autumn Feast of Tabernacles and Jesus entered Jerusalem to the waving of palm branches. The strong and steady palm tree at Christ Church could tell many stories from the drama of history, yet it still bears fruit.

We each have a story to tell and have each seen many changes that have happened around us. In this life, we will never fully know the fruit of our own lives. Every one of us can look back with thanks for something in our past and we still have opportunities to bear fruit today. For some that might be in an active way, and for others it might be in stillness and prayer, remembering those who care for us and those we love.

■ PRAYER

Dear Lord, remind us of things we can give thanks for in our lives yesterday and today. Amen

Song of Solomon 4:3 (NIV)

Love the pomegranate

Your lips are like a scarlet ribbon; your mouth is lovely. Your temples behind your veil are like the halves of a pomegranate.

Pomegranates are common in Israel and are frequently cultivated. The plant is a small shrub, the flowers are red and the fruit is round and multicoloured: pink, yellow and purple. Each fruit has many seeds; the rabbis reckon there are 613, one for each of the commandments of the law. Pomegranates often symbolise fruitfulness and fertility.

Ornamental pomegranates were used on some of the priestly garments and were engraved as decorations in the temple in Jerusalem. They are also found in the love poem, the Song of Solomon or Song of Songs. In chapter 4, a man describes a woman in a glowing and poetic way. The word 'temples' could also be translated 'cheeks'. The book is often taken to be an allegory for the love of God for his people.

As we grow older, love takes on a different meaning. We may not be quite as passionate as we once were (but we might be!). We may have lost a loved one some years ago, but still love them with all our heart. Love between people changes over time. But one thing never, ever changes and that is the love of God.

■ **PRAYER**

Lord God, we thank you for loving us even when we are far from perfect. Show us how to love you more. Amen

Revelation 22:2b (NIV)

Tree of life

On each side of the river stood the tree of life, bearing twelve crops of fruit, yielding its fruit every month. And the leaves of the tree are for the healing of the nations.

The most famous tree in the Bible is the tree of life. We find it in Genesis 3:24, where God protects it from humans after the fall because its fruit gives eternal life. It appears in Proverbs 3:18, where it is linked to wisdom. Then, it is finally found in Revelation as trees on either side of the river of life, coming out of the new Jerusalem. It bears a different fruit each month and its leaves are 'for the healing of the nations'.

When we are young, we may believe that our generation could change the world to be a more peaceful, equitable place. When we look at the global tensions as older people, we realise that no generation has been able to end war and bring healing. Jesus promises that, one day, he will return to bring in the new creation where conflict will be no more.

Meanwhile, we can pray for healing and, as Christ's body, for the church to be those healing leaves to those around us. We find this is no utopia but a practical way of living that makes the future real in the present.

■ **PRAYER**

Heavenly Father, help us to look to your new creation and to point towards it in all that we do. Amen

In remembrance of me

Katherine Hedderly

In autumn, the rhythm of the natural world invites us to enter into a time of renewal in our lives. We wonder at the beauty of the colour of falling leaves, even if we might not be the ones running and catching them these days. The earth takes stock; we give thanks for the fruitfulness of nature and are reminded of how we are to care for creation. After the autumn equinox, the days get shorter and we feel the world turning towards the deepest part of the year. It is a time of reflection and remembrance. If we embrace this time, we are given the opportunity to enjoy the riches of our lives and our world, past and present. This remembering gives us confidence for the future, whatever our stage of life.

The church's year follows the same theme as this rich season, leading us through Harvest, All Saints, All Souls and Remembrancetide. Along the way, we gather up the treasure of our lives – those we have loved, the saints of our own day and those who have gone before us – and come to see the people around us and the natural world with renewed appreciation. All is gift indeed.

Psalm 67:5–6 (NRSV)

Abundance

Let the peoples praise you, O God; let all the peoples praise you. The earth has yielded its increase; God, our God, has blessed us.

Do you, like me, find it hard to trust in God's provision? When Moses led the Israelites through the wilderness, they received manna to eat day by day. It was all that they needed. But when they forgot about God's attentive care and tried to stockpile, things went wrong. All the way through the Bible, we hear about God's abundance. But trying to live with the sense that all will be well isn't easy. We also try to hoard up what we are given, just in case. Particularly as we reach older age, we might want to do that to protect ourselves for what can feel like a fearful future.

What would it mean to live with an awareness of God's abundance rather than a fear of scarcity? At harvest, we're invited to look at the world in this way and it can help us to have that sense of thankfulness in our own lives too. We reap the reward of long friendships, of interests and hobbies that have brought us joy over the years, of all the small things of our lives which, when taken together, remind us that we really are blessed.

■ PRAYER

Lord, at harvest time I remember your love and care for all your creation. Give me a heart that cherishes your gifts. Show me how to live gently and thankfully, in a way that creates abundance for all. Amen

Lamentations 3:22–23 (NRSV)

God's garden

The steadfast love of the Lord never ceases, his mercies never come to an end; they are new every morning; great is your faithfulness.

I once discovered gardeners dismantling the most beautiful border in St James's Park. It had been a riot of colour and a rich texture of wonderful flowers all through the summer, as if earlier in the year someone had decided to tip out every single packet of seed and see what would happen. But now they were taking up each flower and shrub and clearing the ground. A few moments before, there was life and colour, and then everything was gone, leaving bare, empty earth.

Such signs of transformation, all around us in this season, can naturally lead us to reflect. They remind us of the endings we experience in our lives as we face the loss of a loved one, or a change in circumstances. Then we too experience the barren earth, where once the garden had been.

How does God meet us in this place? Often, he meets us in remembering. We remember the life we shared with our loved ones, all the colour and texture of it, and our remembrance bears the seeds of God's kingdom. Like a garden, God's life and love take deep root in the bare earth, and one day we will gaze on the garden of God's eternal beauty and be part of it.

■ **PRAYER**

Lord, when the seasons in my life change, help me to plant seeds of hope in all I am experiencing. Give me patience and trust to wait for your new life to come and grow in me. Amen

1 John 3:2 (NRSV)

Saints remembered

Beloved, we are God's children now; what we will be has not yet been revealed. What we do know is this: when he is revealed, we will be like him, for we will see him as he is.

A saint is anyone who is a friend of God: a friend whose way of life reflects the love and freedom of God with such transparency that their lives become God's invitation to friendship for others. Think of the 'saints' that have made the greatest impression on you and what their friendship with God meant to them. I think of St Francis, who became God's friend through the beauty of creation; of Dietrich Bonhoeffer, living out that deep friendship with Christ in prison day by day; of the assassinated Archbishop Óscar Romero; and of brave, 'ordinary' Christians in the Middle East today.

Being a friend of God doesn't mean being a spiritual giant; it means being able to live our lives honestly with God, being real with God, allowing God to see us as we are, love us and use us, with all our gifts and faults. As we get older, we know only too well what those faults are. It's through them that God's affection shines.

Our friendship with God is made in the ordinary experiences of life. That's the place where friendship is forged and saints are created.

■ **PRAYER**

Lord, you know I'm not perfect but you count me as a friend. As we journey together, make our friendship a way for others to see what life with you is like. Amen

1 Corinthians 13:4–7 (NRSV, abridged)

Enduring love

Love is patient; love is kind; love is not envious or boastful or arrogant or rude… It does not rejoice in wrongdoing, but rejoices in the truth. It bears all things, believes all things, hopes all things, endures all things.

My grandmother always had a photo of my grandfather, Reg, by her on the mantelpiece. She had lost him when he was just 40 years old and she was left to bring up two small girls aged five and two by herself. So I never got to meet him. My mother, who was that little five-year-old, says she has sometimes felt his comforting presence by her side during her life. Through her and my grandmother's remembrances of him, I also feel connected to Reg. There is a sense that that love has continued to be shared by us all, a greater love through which, one day, we will all be together.

Paul has a wonderful way of describing this kind of love that links us. He says it bears, believes, hopes and endures all things. That's the kind of love that we hold on to as the church remembers All Souls in special services. It's a great honour to read out the names of those who have died in the last year and those whom we particularly want to remember.

■ PRAYER

Lord, give us the simplicity to know that we are connected by your love, now and always. As I remember those whom I love and no longer see, show me how to live with the confidence that in you we will be together forever. Amen

1 Kings 19:11b–12 (NRSV)

Holding silence

Now there was a great wind, so strong that it was splitting mountains and breaking rocks in pieces before the Lord, but the Lord was not in the wind; and after the wind an earthquake, but the Lord was not in the earthquake; and after the earthquake a fire, but the Lord was not in the fire; and after the fire a sound of sheer silence.

At Remembrancetide, we hold silence to reflect. Silence holds us and binds us together across ages, generations and experience. On Remembrance Sunday, the silence is a place to hold the memory of those lost through war and conflict and those still living with the effects of war. Those effects can last a lifetime; they might be rooted in experiences we lived through ourselves or by those we knew.

The season of remembrance is also a time when our own longing for peace can deepen as we hold together all our differences, and our wounds, with our hope, joy and wonder at the goodness of the world and the beauty we see in one another. It is the silence of God's presence that speaks deeply without words.

Silence creates the sacred space for us to piece together our lives and our collective memory. It is a place of transformation where we can remember the past and where the future comes to birth.

■ PRAYER

Drop thy still dews of quietness,
Till all our strivings cease;
Take from our souls the strain and stress,
And let our ordered lives confess
*The beauty of thy peace.**

* John Greenleaf Whittier (1807–92)

Matthew 25:35, 40 (NRSV, abridged)

Remembering others

For I was hungry and you gave me food, I was thirsty and you gave me something to drink, I was a stranger and you welcomed me… Truly I tell you, just as you did it to one of the least of these… you did it to me.

St Martin was a Roman soldier of the fourth century. One winter's night, he encountered a destitute man at the city gate. Out of concern for him, he took his own cloak, divided it in two and gave half to the man to keep him warm. That night in a dream, he saw the beggar coming towards him, and as he looked at his face he recognised Christ.

Jesus tells his disciples that, in remembering the needs of others, they will meet him. This turns every act of kindness into a place where we can encounter Jesus. When the circumstances of our lives mean that we aren't as active as we once were, we might not think that we have a cloak to share. But God still transforms our every gesture and offering.

One woman in our congregation, who lives with a disability, knits warm hats for the members of our Sunday International Group, who are all refugees, asylum seekers or homeless here in London. That's the 'cloak' that she shares. What might yours be?

■ PRAYER

Lord, I know that you are alongside all those who are in need. Show me who you want me to remember today. Amen

Luke 2:43–45 (NRSV)

Living with hope

When the festival was ended and they started to return, the boy Jesus stayed behind in Jerusalem, but his parents did not know it. Assuming that he was in the group of travellers, they went a day's journey. Then they started to look for him among their relatives and friends. When they did not find him, they returned to Jerusalem to search for him.

Every year at this time, we hold a service at St Martin-in-the-Fields for the families of those who are missing. Theirs are heartbreaking stories of loss and waiting but also of courage and love. A few years ago, some members of the families formed a choir and it has gone from strength to strength, including being on national television. Singing in the choir is one way for these families to remember and hold out hope together. In the service, they are the ones to light candles and share that light around the whole church.

We often light candles as a sign of the hope we have: light to guide us and show us the way; light in the darkness of worry and concern; a candle lit for someone we remember with love.

Mary and Joseph find Jesus in the temple, in his Father's house. We can only imagine the relief that they felt. You might be holding out hope for someone as you remember them today. Allow God to remind you that he holds out hope too. A candle burns in God's heart for each one of us.

■ **PRAYER**

Lord, lift my heart to know that the flame of your love is constant, bringing light and hope to the whole world. Amen

1 Corinthians 12:24b–27 (NRSV, abridged)

Re-membered

God has so arranged the body... that there may be no dissension within the body... If one member suffers, all suffer together with it; if one member is honoured, all rejoice together with it. Now you are the body of Christ and individually members of it.

Our life with God begins with remembrance. The people of Israel renewed their relationship with God as they remembered all that he had done for them. His loving forgiveness gave them a way to journey on faithfully. We come, weak and strong, of different ages and abilities, different backgrounds, cultures and life experiences and are re-membered as we gather around the person of Jesus. 'Do this in remembrance of me,' he said, and so we are formed into a new community at the Eucharist, through bread and wine.

One of the characteristics of that community is love for one another. In our culture today, which is often so focused on the individual, having a real concern and care for others, particularly for the weakest among us, is life-giving. In Jesus, we are held as one. We suffer as one. We rejoice as one.

When you are feeling at your weakest, can you imagine that you are being remembered by Jesus, as the most precious part of his community?

■ **PRAYER**

Lord, whether I feel strong or weak today, may I experience the comfort of being part of your family. Amen

John 6:35, 37 (NRSV)

Just as I am

Jesus said to them, 'I am the bread of life. Whoever comes to me will never be hungry, and whoever believes in me will never be thirsty… Everything that the Father gives me will come to me, and anyone who comes to me I will never drive away.'

In the autumn, we have held a Disability Conference at St Martin-in-the-Fields for the last six years. Each year, we welcome those with lived experience of disability to take part, as we do theology together. Speaking about God through the experience of disability helps the church to grow and become more the community that God calls us to be. We say we are an inclusive church, but what that means in practice is about being a place where everyone is accepted, just as they are.

Jesus invites us to remember who we are, in the light of his own 'I Am' sayings, found in John's gospel. We are each invited to live out our own 'I Am'. God takes us just as we are, as Charlotte Elliott, the writer of the famous hymn, knew only too well, having lived with illness for a large part of her life. That can be challenging for us, when we begin to lose some of our agility, memory or health. Who is the 'I Am' that God is calling today?

■ PRAYER

Just as I am, thy love unknown,
has broken every barrier down;
now to be thine, yea, thine alone,
O Lamb of God, I come.*

* Charlotte Elliott (1789–1871)

Ephesians 1:17–18 (NRSV)

Faithful king

I pray that the God of our Lord Jesus Christ, the Father of glory, may give you a spirit of wisdom and revelation as you come to know him, so that, with the eyes of your heart enlightened, you may know what is the hope to which he has called you, what are the riches of his glorious inheritance among the saints.

The feast of Christ the King comes at the end of the church's year, before we turn to the seasons of Advent and Christmas. We are reminded that it is in Jesus, the servant King, that all our hopes and fears and joys are gathered together. It is an opportunity for us to look back and remember when we have allowed Jesus to be Lord of our lives. We see the ways in which he has been faithful to us and true to his word.

When we allow Christ, the gentle King, to rule in our lives, we remember that he came 'not to be served but to serve' (Matthew 20:28). How might he be nudging us to allow someone to help and serve us, in a way that will give peace of mind, and perhaps a new lease of life? How do we receive that love?

■ PRAYER

Lord, come with your gentle rule into my life. Give me the humility to receive the love, gifts and care of others. Let them be channels of your love, my Lord and my King. Amen

The Gift of Years

Debbie Thrower founded and leads The Gift of Years programme. She has pioneered the Anna Chaplaincy model, offering spiritual care to older people, and is widely involved in training and advocacy. Visit **thegiftofyears.org.uk** to find out more.

Debbie writes…

Welcome to a thought-provoking series of reflections – all of them written by people with long and valuable life experience.

P.D. James once said that some things in life should be firmly relegated to the past: 'They are over and must be accepted, made sense of and forgiven.' Whether we spend time contentedly alone or at risk of spiralling into despair is, to some extent, down to us. Descartes said, famously: 'I think therefore I am,' and in a sense, we *are* what we think.

Few people reach an advanced age without knowing that their resilience (or lack of it) is largely dependent on what memories they allow to linger… or choose to dismiss.

Here, you may find kindred spirits or those with whom you disagree, but I guarantee our writers will prompt interesting reflections of your own as you consider what makes you uniquely YOU. Our conscious thoughts will have a bearing on how we discover our identity as we grow older. It's one of the reasons we fear a loss of memory so much. But if our ability to remember does fade, these writers may console us with the thought that in God's memory we remain safe, always: 'Jesus Christ is the same yesterday and today and forever' (Hebrews 13:8).

Best wishes

Meet Sir Mark Tully

The writer and broadcaster **Mark Tully** has been based in India for over 50 years and was the BBC's correspondent in Delhi until 1994. He continues to write, speak and broadcast, with a series of books, television programmes including *The Lives of Jesus*, and radio programmes including *Something Understood*. He celebrated his 82nd birthday last year and was knighted in 2002. He loves the Anglican Church and steam railways.

Retirement seems an alien concept to you. What motivates you to keep going long after most people have put their feet up?

I think, like the rest of my life, it's a matter of drift – work keeps on coming in, so one might as well do it. I've often thought that, living in India, I should metaphorically close down and go into the forest to meditate and prepare for the end – and I dare say I will eventually – but so long as the work keeps coming in, I'll just go on doing it.

Do you understand the work you do – broadcasting, writing, speaking – as a vocation in the same way as if you'd followed an earlier career path and continued with your ordination training in Cambridge?

No, I don't see it as a vocation – I think that would be putting it too highly. I see it as something in part that has simply come my way, but I do see it as an opportunity to say things that I believe in. Whether or not anyone pays any attention to that, I don't know. And as for my current affairs broadcasting – which is really very limited these days – I stick to what I've always done, which is trying to tell people what I see is happening in the way I see it is happening.

When you were working on your television series *The Lives of Jesus*, and in the early years of *Something Understood*, you said that this work had brought you back to your Anglican roots. What did you mean by that?

Well, I was very far from my Anglican roots at a certain period in my life. I was not going to church, not saying prayers, not doing any of the things I should have been doing. I wasn't doing this deliberately; I wasn't saying I reject all this Anglican stuff, I just drifted away. These two programmes coming together, and reading theology again and being involved, meeting wonderful Anglicans, I realised that a huge part of my life was associated with the church and I remembered how much it had meant to me as a young man. Now, I don't have that youthful fervour any longer but I always say, and I absolutely mean it, that I hope to die a member of the Anglican faith.

How would you describe the influence that 50 years of living in India has had on your faith and your beliefs?

Of course, India has had a huge impact – I've found it impossible to live in India and take an interest in the life of India and the religion of India and go on believing that Christianity is the only way to God, which is what I'd been brought up to believe. So India has convinced me that there are different ways to God – the Jains would say there are different ways to the mountaintop. That is really the big difference that India has made to my faith and beliefs, and inevitably that has forced me to think about many aspects of the church, for instance to wonder about its missionary work. Again, I was brought up to believe that we should be spreading the gospel and winning converts, but now I think, do you want to go around undermining other peoples' faith and interfering with their religious life? I'm not sure that you do.

Yet you've had at least two very good friends who were missionary priests – Father Ian and Father Roger – men who gave a lifetime of service to what they would have understood as the mission field in India.

They were both wonderful men and they both had a great love for India, right up to the moment of their deaths. What I admired about them was the way that, despite so many setbacks to what they must have originally believed in, they had a faith that sustained them through all the problems and disappointments. Neither of them had a faith which was aggressive or purblind, it was just a profound certainty.

Having celebrated your 82nd birthday, what does the phrase 'The Gift of Years' conjure up for you?

Well, if you follow my rather eccentric philosophy, you would see good and bad in everything. And yes, there is a huge gift in age. There's the gift of being able in a way to throw off a lot of responsibilities. All those years spent striving to get on, to make more money or whatever – you realise how futile a lot of that was. In that way, age is a gift, but there is a sorrow and a suffering in age as well. As you look back over your life, you see so many things you're ashamed of, so many things you're sorry about, and so many people you miss. And the older you get, the more the threat of loneliness is very real. If you're honest, those you're closest to are the people of your own generation – at least, that's how I feel. I love my children very much, but I couldn't honestly say I'm as close to them as I am to some of my closest friends of my own age.

Andrew Rudd lives in Frodsham, Cheshire. This poem was written when he was Cheshire Poet Laureate in 2006. He is currently Poet in Residence at Manchester Cathedral. He has taught poetry and creative writing, and teaches about spirituality to ordinands and trainee Readers in the Church of England.

This is how it will be

*You will open your eyes
in the morning, and the world
will run to you in its best suit.*

*Trees will make shadow-plays
with their fingers. Creatures
will call out their names.*

*You will open your ears to music
no one has heard before, voices of those
you love and those who love you,*

*the highest note and the deep note
which is only a stirring in the earth. You will
open your mouth, and the things you will say*

*will be old words in new shapes.
Your stories will weave all the threads
into one cloth. You will open*

*your hand, scatter bread for birds,
give to those who have nothing to give.
Your hand will take hold of another hand*

*and walk into a new world,
which is your world, and our world, and we
will be behind you.*

Andrew Rudd (used with kind permission)

Meet the writers: the Hodsons

Margot is Rector of six churches in Buckinghamshire and has been involved in working with the environment since she was a student. **Martin** is a scientist, originally a plant scientist. He's worked on environment and faith for about 25 years and is now the Operations Director with the John Ray Initiative, a charity looking at combining faith and the environment. They regularly work together, each covering both scientific and theological aspects of the environment. Why, we wondered, did they decide to write about trees?

Margot: Trees are very important to the natural world, they're important in the Bible – there are lots of places in the Bible where particular trees are mentioned – and they also illustrate all sorts of spiritual truths, lessons God is teaching us. I've always loved trees. It was probably Dutch elm disease that really got me thinking about ecological problems back in the 1970s when I was at school. That's something that has always stayed with me.

Martin: I've always loved trees too and I've written quite a number of scientific papers about them. The first one concerned a poor beech tree in Wales that was being poisoned by road salt dumped under it.

How does your faith drive and shape your environmental work?

Martin: For me, two of my main work roles are in the field of faith and environment. The John Ray Initiative is an organisation which was set up to look at the interaction between Christianity and the environment, so it's a central part of my work.

Margot: My faith is very much informed by my understanding of the environment and my understanding of the environment is very much informed by my faith. It's believing in God who is creator, and who sees his creation as good, and believing in the Holy Spirit who is sustainer, and sustains this beautiful world that God has created, and in Jesus who is redeemer, who has redeemed the whole world through all that he did for us on the cross.

We will one day see that redemption fully, as we look towards a remade heaven and earth when all things will be renewed and creation will no longer be groaning, as it talks about in Romans 8, and the leaves of the trees will be for the healing of the nations, as it talks about in Revelation 22. And the idea that the whole gospel is for the whole world – the whole universe – is something I find quite mind-blowing and that drives my understanding of nature. It also drives my understanding of the gospel when I see the world that God has made.

You both have experience working across a wide range of age groups: can you generalise at all about how the different generations are dealing with environmental issues?

Margot: I think it's not as straightforward as some people might say. Some people seem to have this stereotype that older people are carbon-guzzling, let's-forget-about-the-planet dinosaurs and young people are deep-green, vegan carrot-eaters. And it's not like that at all. It's much more of a broad range across the board and, just as post-modernism affected all age groups, not just the young, I think all age groups have been affected by the things people see happening in the environment. People are people, and people respond in different ways, in different age groups and different socio-economic groups, but the general pattern in this country is towards increasing awareness.

Martin: When I did the 'The Hope of Planet Earth' tours with Tearfund and A Rocha UK some years ago and we spoke to schools, they were largely 16-year-olds. Quite a lot of them were really committed, but there was also quite a lot of apathy and, sadly, there were some who seem to have been 'over-cooked' on environmentalism at school and were just saying, 'We're all going to die, it's too late to do anything about it, so let's just live and be merry.' So in my experience, it isn't as clear-cut as saying older people aren't environmentally friendly and young people are – it doesn't work like that.

Is there anything else either of you would like to add?

Margot: We have a U3A [University of the Third Age] in our village and also some older clubs which are much more traditional – the kind of clubs that people in their 60s used to join, but things have changed enormously since those sorts of clubs were set up. People in their 60s and 70s and even into their 80s are very much more active than they used to be even a generation ago. They join cycling clubs rather than lunch clubs, and we joke that there's probably a U3A white-water rafting group. So we've seen a huge change in the activity levels and energy levels of older people.

Martin: I'm on the U3A speaker circuit and I speak quite often to them. In Haddenham, there are so many people attached to U3A that there's nowhere big enough to hold them all so they have to run all the meetings twice. The questions you get after a talk are always very sharp: thoughtful and well-informed.

Margot: And we hear similar stories from all over the area.

The gift of play

Anne Townsend

My 80-year-old mother could contain her bewilderment no longer. 'We've just bought all this beautiful fabric, but now you're going to take it home, chop it up and then stitch it together again. What a waste!'

How could I help her understand that cutting, selecting shapes and colours, and arranging the fabrics was, for me, wonderfully creative relaxation? I took a deep breath and muttered, 'It's worker's play-time!' Our minds returned to my wartime childhood, and the fun we shared together when we stopped 'working' and listened or danced to the two hours of music on the wireless. She got it at once.

Neuroscientists tell us that the areas of the brain triggered by playing and creativity are also close to that part which responds to religious stimuli. Creativity can deepen our spiritual awareness and draw us closer to God.

In these reflections, I hope you'll enjoy thinking about some of the different aspects of playing, of creativity and of games that I discovered in the Bible. We are supposed to be in our 'second childhood'. Childhood is, above all, a God-given time when we can 'play' – and pray – without pressure that 'we ought to be working'.

Genesis 1:31a; 2:1–2 (RSV)

Creating and making

And God saw everything that he had made, and behold, it was very good… Thus the heavens and the earth were finished, and all the host of them. And on the seventh day God finished his work which he had done.

We read about God's 'work' in creation, but there's another side to it. This must have been such fun. It reminds me of 'play' – which is defined as being 'what children and young people do when they follow their own ideas and interests, in their own way, and for their own reasons': a brilliant description of what I imagine God was doing when he made not only our universe but also everything beyond it. God was playing!

For many of us, a bonus of attaining our 'second childhood' is that we gain the opportunity of using our imaginative and creative selves in totally new ways. God-given talents and gifts may surface completely unexpectedly. We may find we can paint, write poetry, grow plants, sing in a pop choir, play the harp, take and edit photos on smartphones or fill the garden with washing-up liquid bubbles.

We who are made in God's image may rediscover a long-forgotten gift of play. Yes, God is concerned with the heavy, sad and serious stuff of our lives. But our God is also the God who plays, and we were designed to be like him.

■ **PRAYER**

Playful God, in my second childhood, may I cherish the gifts of play you now offer me as much as I did in my first. Amen

Zechariah 8:5 (ESV)

Heaven's children

And the streets of the city shall be full of boys and girls playing in its streets.

Aged 101, my mother longed to be reunited with her son, who died as a baby during World War II. She wondered, 'Will he still be a baby, or has he grown up?' How could I answer? My best attempt was, 'I'm sure his arms are wide open just waiting for your special hug,' and then we'd laugh together.

This was not the moment to discuss theological concepts and how our linear notions of time don't work when it comes to eternity. In God's eternity, our past, present and future are blended together into complete wholeness. What happens after death is described in picture language in the Bible and we don't have precise details to satisfy our rational minds.

But we can know that heaven in the Bible is definitely a place of peace, security, safety and contentment. There are no out-of-control juggernauts, abductors, tsunamis or other dangers to prevent us, children, playing in her streets. It seems we will play heavenly versions of hopscotch, tag and 'follow my leader' to our heart's content.

We can look forward to facing the great unknown of heaven knowing that God, who loves us greatly, has prepared something amazingly wonderful for us.

■ **PRAYER**

Welcoming God, please help me to face my ultimate destiny with trust and confidence in you. Amen

Psalm 33:2–3 (NIV)

Play joyfully

Praise the Lord with the harp; make music to him on the ten-stringed lyre. Sing to him a new song; play skilfully, and shout for joy.

The psalmist encourages us to praise and wonder at our marvellous God. When we joyfully flourish as Christians, basking in God's nearness, this is easy. When God seems a trillion miles away, and life seems harsh and totally unfair, we struggle.

At times like this, God's gift of play helps me. I like the saying that play is 'what children and young people do when they're not being told what to do by adults'. In later life, many of us find ourselves released from the shackles of making ourselves perform as previously expected. Even fear of failure may loosen its hold on us.

We probably don't wear purple with red, or sit on pavements licking ice creams, but unexpectedly we may feel able to experiment with things we would never have thought possible in our former, carefully structured lives. 'What will others think?' no longer cripples us. I'll never be the 95-year-old granny who abseils down church towers or leaps out of helicopters. My ageing body forbids it. But I can play and experiment with fabrics and my sewing machine, and many unexplored activities like writing poetry, painting, collage and even making my own Christmas cards.

We may also be freed up to discover whether our regular, familiar style of church worship and private prayer still suits us, or whether something different now fits better.

■ **PRAYER**

Joy-filled God, give me the courage to play and experiment and so grow closer to you. Amen

Isaiah 66:12 (ESV)

Great-grandchildren

For thus says the Lord: 'Behold, I will extend peace to her like a river, and the glory of the nations like an overflowing stream; and you shall nurse, you shall be carried upon her hip, and bounced upon her knees.'

More than anything, my husband longs to be a great-grandfather. His face softens gently as he imagines tenderly cradling a tiny new baby in his arms.

God promises each one of us similar nurturing care. We may need reassurance that this is there ready for us, when we go through seemingly endless hours of waiting in hospital, painful medical procedures, reactions to medication and facing losses, emptiness and disappointments.

Remember the look of utter contentment and relaxation on the face of a baby nursing at the breast – this pictures God's provision for us. Remember the toddler being bounced rhythmically on a mother's knee – this is what God promises us. Think of the child carried safe and close on a mother's hip. God promises us that too.

God's loving care is offered wholly and without condition. It no more depends on me having faith that God will supply than a crying baby requires faith that mother will feed her.

God speaks in terms of 'a river' and 'an overflowing stream'. Those of us who grew up during the war will remember rationing and shortages. But God uses the language of plenty. There is more than enough to go around. We are loved and held; we will be replete.

■ **PRAYER**

Nurturing God, thank you that you will always look after me. Amen

Luke 9:46–48 (NIV, abridged)

Small – beautiful

An argument started… as to which of them would be the greatest. Jesus, knowing their thoughts, took a little child and… said to them, 'Whoever welcomes this little child in my name welcomes me; and whoever welcomes me welcomes the one who sent me. For it is the one who is least among you all who is the greatest.'

Tigger-like, my 70-year-old friend exclaimed, 'It's great to be eight inside!' We had just celebrated by breakfasting on half a cherry tomato each – the first we had ever grown. Dancing with delight in something as mundane as a little tomato is a far cry from a lifetime of heavy-duty professional and family responsibility.

Back in 1373, Mother Julian shared one of her famous visions: '[Jesus] showed me a little thing, the size of a hazelnut, lying in the palm of my hand, as it seemed to me, and it was round as a ball. I looked at it with my mind's eye and thought, "What can this be?" And the answer came in a general way, like this: "It is all that is made."' Her visions gave Julian a profound confidence that, cradled in God's love, 'All shall be well, and all shall be well, and all manner of thing shall be well.'

In our later years, importance becomes unimportant, status and income lose their significance, and we marvel that our supreme value lies in being cherished by God.

■ **PRAYER**

God of security, help me to value your unconditional love. Amen

Matthew 19:14 (NIV)

Not me

Jesus said, 'Let the little children come to me, and do not hinder them, for the kingdom of heaven belongs to such as these.'

'They treat me as if I'm a three-year-old imbecile,' weeps Sarah, tottering along on her walking frame. 'They don't respect me and snigger behind my back.' On the other side of the room, a former university professor is being spoon-fed lunch and no one knows that his scientific discoveries once made him internationally famous.

Many of us dread the discovery that we have been reclassified. It is as if we have turned into helpless children overnight, instead of others seeing us for the people we really are inside. We shy away from 'has-beens'.

Developing dementia is, for many of us, the greatest fear. We dread losing those essential ingredients that make us our unique selves. Will our real, familiar self be totally forgotten? Used to self-sufficiency, we fear becoming as needy as little children.

But Jesus makes it clear that the characteristics of small children make them treasured in his kingdom. He does not say that those capable of 'going it alone' are of special merit. Rather, supreme value is placed on each one of us who (to the rest of the world) appears to be like a dependent toddler. If only we could grasp and glory in this reversal of our previous values and norms.

■ **PRAYER**

God of the needy, make me unafraid to be whoever I am becoming. Amen

Hebrews 12:1b–3 (NIV, abridged)

Second chance race

Let us run with perseverance the race marked out for us, fixing our eyes on Jesus, the pioneer and perfecter of faith… Consider him… so that you will not grow weary and lose heart.

Monday mornings, in my retirement home, sees a gaggle of residents sitting in a circle, precariously waving water-filled plastic bottles in time to music. Some 90-year-olds reckon those 'exercises' are comparable to the Paralympics. Were any of them to try carrying those heavy bottles to the shops, I might intervene to dissuade them.

As children develop, they stop playing 'tag' just for fun. Those who go on to be professional athletes rid themselves of all unnecessary weights and even wear especially streamlined outfits.

So why do some of us persist in carrying unnecessary weights around as we head for home? God encourages us not to weigh ourselves down with guilt, regret, resentment and anger, as we head for the finishing line. Some internal baggage could be thrown off. There may be time to eat humble pie and right some wrongs.

My friend lived for years regretting his part in getting his manager sacked. Late in life, he was able to contact each person involved. He expressed his regret and asked for forgiveness. Another friend ended a lifetime's family feud by apologising to her estranged brother. We haven't reached the end quite yet. We still have time. We may still have a second chance.

■ **PRAYER**

Forgiving God, help me to play your way and to be the one to say, 'I'm sorry!' Amen

Isaiah 35:1, 3–4a (NIV, abridged)

Being myself

The desert and the parched land will be glad; the wilderness will rejoice and blossom… Strengthen the feeble hands, steady the knees that give way; say to those with fearful hearts, 'Be strong, do not fear.'

Something important happens when we play and connect with our creative selves. Psychologists suggest that playing is a way of being yourself and knowing yourself. Children discover who they are when they play unrestrictedly.

Some of us feel our lives are unbearably cramped by the limitations of age. We can barely turn over in bed, let alone actively play or create anything. We are familiar with bone-dry deserts – that's how we feel inside. Sitting passively in front of the television, for days on end, dulls our minds and shrivels up our spirits.

God speaks of life bursting forth in restricted situations. Creativity does not necessarily require mobile bodies and agile minds. We can create patterns from cracks on the ceiling, invent stories about the people surrounding us, sing to ourselves and dance our fingers and toes to our silent music. We discover who we now are, who we have become, as we play in the unfamiliar deserts called 'Old Age'.

Like the sunflower seed, which rooted and blossomed in a derelict bomb site, we raise our heads high, for it is in this place that God promises, 'Be strong, do not fear.'

■ **PRAYER**

Give me the courage to see and to be the person I now am. Amen

Exodus 31:3–6 (RSV, abridged)

Creative gifts

I have filled [Bezalel] with the Spirit of God, with ability and intelligence, with knowledge and all craftsmanship, to devise artistic designs... for work in every craft... And I have given to all able people ability that they may make all that I have commanded you.

Picturing the great temple Solomon built may defy our imagination. We read about the plethora of crafts and intricate designs incorporated. Perhaps we notice for the first time that a Spirit-filled man was essential to oversee this massive, creative enterprise.

We may think of those who preach and evangelise as being filled with the Holy Spirit. Yet God talks about creativity requiring Spirit-filled people.

My friend cannot leave her wheelchair. She can, however, use her camera. Every day, she posts a unique photograph on Facebook. These are no ordinary pictures. She tries to see and capture our world from God's perspective. Her close-ups are my favourites. They capture the sap-swelling leaf veins, a drop of water about to burst and sunlight seesawing over the brim of a cup. Her creativity wordlessly introduces her Facebook friends to the God who sees differently and gives her restricted life, and ours, joyful meaning.

When we create in any way, we often sense God's gentle breath and nearness. This is why one person says, 'I'm close to God in my garden.' And another, 'Playing with patchwork is praying.'

■ **PRAYER**

Gentle but strong God, set me free for your life and love to flow through my creativity. Amen

Matthew 11:16–19a (NRSV, abridged)

The different game

[This generation] is like children… calling to one another, 'We played the flute for you, and you did not dance; we wailed, and you did not mourn.' For John came neither eating nor drinking, and they say, 'He has a demon'; the Son of Man came eating and drinking, and they say, 'Look, a glutton and a drunkard, a friend of tax-collectors and sinners!'

I got married to my teddy bear about 15 times, in the game my brother and I used to play years ago. We played the same game, with the same rules, and it worked. But Jesus teaches that, no matter whether it was himself or John the Baptist, his hearers were dissatisfied. They refused to play with him.

Let's face it, it's often us 'vintage' church members who aren't great at playing 'church' in its current form. We prefer things the old way.

I wish you could have been at my church's holiday club for 65 children aged between five and eleven. Three of us 'nearly and over-80s' were team leaders. We offered wisdom and experience. Teenage 'junior leaders' supported us. Not only were they highly mobile, but their hands could cut and shape in seconds – while arthritic fingers like mine took minutes.

It wasn't 'Do it my way!', 'No, mine's better!' We pooled our resources and played together to build God's church of the future.

I'll tell you a secret: I even managed to dance without falling over and I painted a unicorn.

■ **PRAYER**

God who plays with us all, may we never hold back our church as she dances into your future. Amen

Friends for life

Roger Combes

What can I expect in a good friend? What can a friend expect from me? Is a friend just someone I enjoy spending time with? Are there obligations in a friendship, as in other relationships, or is the whole point of a friendship that duty is absent?

At some time or another, most of us have known friendship as one of life's joys, something that has been greatly supportive and enriching. A 'friend' can take many forms, and friendship can enhance the life of the smallest child or the oldest adult. But desirable as friendship may be, it can be elusive and complicated.

In the following pages, we shall see a range of friendships. As always, the Bible is rich and practical in its stories and observations. Here are men and women of God, old and young, from acquaintances to neighbours to friends 'who stick closer than a brother' (Proverbs 18:24, NIV), being friends and reflecting on the importance of friendship in their often-difficult lives.

Ecclesiastes 4:9–12 (NIV, abridged)

It's what friends do

Two are better than one, because they have a good return for their labour: if either of them falls down, one can help the other up... If two lie down together, they will keep warm... Though one may be overpowered, two can defend themselves. A cord of three strands is not quickly broken.

It's not rocket science, as the saying goes. Two climbers find themselves in a sudden blizzard, cut off, lost and freezing; they have to wait until help comes or the weather clears. In a single tent, and even a single sleeping bag, together they can preserve enough body heat to survive the night. Similarly, a soldier injured in battle knows his mates will get him back to base. Or again, everyone knows walking home in the dark is safer with a friend. Life was as problematic in the ancient world as it is today but, as these verses show, then as now, we are less vulnerable when we have someone alongside. It's 'better'.

Not everyone finds it easy being friends with someone. It means having to be more flexible and less selfish, and perhaps losing a little freedom. Friendships can be harder to make as we get older and perhaps more set in our ways. But as the writer of Ecclesiastes well knew, the riches of true friendship far outweigh the costs: mutual company and support, advice and different points of view, comfort when cold winds blow, even some laughs. It's what friends do.

■ **PRAYER**

Lord Jesus, thank you for the enrichment and enjoyment that friends bring to our lives. Amen

1 Samuel 23:15–17a (NIV)

David and Jonathan (1)

While David was at Horesh in the Desert of Ziph, he learned that Saul had come out to take his life. And Saul's son Jonathan went to David at Horesh and helped him find strength in God. 'Don't be afraid,' he said. 'My father Saul will not lay a hand on you. You shall be king over Israel, and I will be second to you.'

Laurel and Hardy, Morecambe and Wise, the Two Ronnies and many others. We laugh and enjoy the fun: great double acts, perfect partnerships, at least on screen.

David and Jonathan's friendship is perhaps the best known in the Bible. They had much in common. Both were daring fighters and both were men of principle, deeply committed to the Lord's ways and purposes. Both were loyal to the flawed King Saul, Jonathan's father.

Jonathan might have expected to inherit the throne but, completely without resentment, he fully supported David as the royal heir. Jonathan was a voice of practical wisdom for David, both at court and in private conversation. Here, Jonathan sought out David in the desert when David was in great danger from Saul, and 'strengthened his hand in God' (AMP). Jonathan is a fine model for us. His many-layered friendship brought David empathy, a coming alongside, a promise of loyalty and renewed trust in God. Such a friend is very precious and, as the old hymn says, we have just such a friend in Jesus.

■ **PRAYER**

Help us, Lord, to be wise and loyal friends. Amen

1 Samuel 18:1, 3; 2 Samuel 1:25–26 (NIV, abridged)

David and Jonathan (2)

Jonathan became one in spirit with David, and he loved him as himself… And Jonathan made a covenant with David… 'How the mighty have fallen in battle! Jonathan lies slain on your heights. I grieve for you, Jonathan my brother; you were very dear to me. Your love for me was wonderful, more wonderful than that of women.'

I wonder when David realised that Jonathan was such an exceptional and wonderful friend. Let's hope it was well before Jonathan's untimely death. Generally, we don't hear much of David expressing love or appreciation to others around him, except in his psalms praising the Lord. But when he heard the news from the battlefront that Jonathan had died, he spoke freely of his love for Jonathan and Jonathan's love for him. Sadly, sometimes we only recognise people's qualities after we have lost them, when it is too late to tell them of our affection and indebtedness.

Jonathan was the one who took the lead in this friendship: he had initiated it in the first place and he was always generous in spirit and in deed. 'Give and take' is at the heart of most good friendships, but Jonathan seemed to go further, being happy to give without getting so much in return. Do we give as much as we take in our friendships?

■ PRAYER

Lord, help us to recognise and appreciate our friends and their qualities. Help us to tell them what they mean to us while we still have the chance. Amen

John 11: 1, 3, 5, 33, 36 (NIV, abridged)

Friends Jesus loved

A man named Lazarus was ill. He was from Bethany, the village of Mary and her sister Martha… So the sisters sent word to Jesus, 'Lord, the one you love is ill…' Now Jesus loved Martha and her sister and Lazarus… When Jesus saw [Mary] weeping… he was deeply moved in spirit and troubled… Then the Jews said, 'See how he loved them!'

'They are very close.' Two friends know each other and understand each other very well. Somehow, they recognise a kindred spirit in the other. Despite their differences, they are completely at ease in the other's company. It is a rather beautiful thing.

The friendship between Jesus and the small family of Mary, Martha and Lazarus seems to have been a close one. Four times in one chapter, we are told that Jesus loved them. In the story, Mary and Martha talk with Jesus with openness and trust; and surely Jesus found their home a place where he was accepted and understood, and where he could relax and enjoy hospitality. This mutual friendship would grow closer still as, in the coming verses, Jesus raised their brother Lazarus from the dead and Mary anointed Jesus publicly with her precious ointment. Our Lord Jesus was very human and he loved his friends.

■ **PRAYER**

For the joy of human love…
Friends below and friends above,
Christ, our God, to you we raise
*This our sacrifice of praise.**

* Folliott S. Pierpoint (1835–1917)

Colossians 4:7, 10–12, 14 (NIV, abridged)

Paul's home group

Tychicus will tell you all the news about me. He is a dear brother, a faithful minister and fellow servant in the Lord… My fellow prisoner Aristarchus sends you his greetings, as does Mark… They have proved a comfort to me. Epaphras, who is one of you and a servant of Christ Jesus, sends greetings… Our dear friend Luke, the doctor, and Demas send greetings.

Some people are brilliant are keeping their friendships in good repair. Arranging to meet up when they can, remembering birthdays with a card or text, making a phone call or sending an email are all worth the effort. Paul kept in contact with friends even when, as here, he was in prison.

And friends were supporting him there. One fellow prisoner, Aristarchus, was a believer and that was a comfort. Young Mark, who did some early mission work with Paul, was a tonic. Tychicus was an ideal prison visitor. Paul describes him appreciatively as a faithful and dear brother and colleague. Dr Luke, whom Paul calls a 'dear friend' (NIV) or 'beloved' (NRSV), was also there, as was Epaphras, a devoted pray-er and support. Paul greatly valued these friends, and said so.

Words are deeds, and they can do great good. Paul gratefully receives encouragement from his companions and he sends on everyone's news and greetings to his friends at Colossae. Friendship is always two-way with Paul.

■ **PRAYER**

Thank you, Lord, for news of friends, family and fellowships, and for those who are their messengers. Help me to be a thoughtful and responsive friend in return. Amen

Proverbs 17:17; 18:24; 27:10a (NIV)

A constant friend

A friend loves at all times, and a brother is born for a time of adversity… One who has unreliable friends soon comes to ruin, but there is a friend who sticks closer than a brother… Do not forsake your friend or a friend of your family.

Hiding in enemy-occupied territory is a perilous business. Across occupied Europe in World War II, many a grounded Allied pilot or escaping prisoner-of-war depended on the extraordinary bravery of local families who gave them food and shelter. Most of all, they needed not to be betrayed. Moving stories abound of resolute local rescuers proving faithful to these foreign friends, protecting and shielding them, despite the huge risks involved.

Being faithful is surely at the heart of friendship. When a friend betrays another, we feel that it is deeply incongruous, a hurtful contradiction. But betrayals aren't only big, life-threatening events. It's possible to betray our friends in the small things too: by a lack of sensitivity or thoughtfulness, or by talking about them behind their backs, or by changing our attitude towards them if their circumstances change, for good or ill. Whatever stage of life we and our friends are at, it can be helpful to do a weather check on ourselves, to make sure we are constant in our friendship.

■ **PRAYER**

Thank you, Lord, for those who have gone out of their way to help me at various times of my life and who have not let me down. Help me in turn to be a constant friend to others. Amen

Luke 1:39b–42, 56 (NIV)

Elizabeth and Mary

[Mary] hurried to a town in the hill country in Judea, where she entered Zechariah's home and greeted Elizabeth. When Elizabeth heard Mary's greeting, the baby leaped in her womb, and Elizabeth was filled with the Holy Spirit. In a loud voice she exclaimed: 'Blessed are you among women and blessed is the child you will bear!'... Mary stayed with Elizabeth for about three months and then returned home.

The house had been quieter in recent months, since Elizabeth's husband Zechariah had lost the power of speech. Elizabeth, remarkably at her advanced age, was expecting a child. They probably kept themselves to themselves. Then suddenly it was all change: talking, singing, rejoicing. Mary, a cousin in her teens from Nazareth, arrived for three months. It was a short but doubtless profound friendship that came at a key time for both Elizabeth and Mary.

What a breath of fresh air Mary must have been for Elizabeth. How encouraging that God was fulfilling his promises in the coming generation. As for Mary, she must have been bursting to have someone to confide in. She could ask Elizabeth all her questions and, with the support of this older, believing couple, Mary could begin to adjust to the wonder and challenge of being the mother of the Son of God.

Young people need friendship and support as they set off into adulthood. Elizabeth enthusiastically affirmed Mary and her calling right from the start. How valuable and important that must have been.

■ PRAYER

Heavenly Father, help me to be a positive and affirming presence for the young people I have contact with, for Jesus' sake. Amen

2 Timothy 4:9–12, 20–21a (NIV)

Friends on the move

Come to me quickly, for Demas, because he loved this world, has deserted me and has gone to Thessalonica. Crescens has gone to Galatia, and Titus to Dalmatia. Only Luke is with me. Get Mark and bring him with you, for he is helpful to me in my ministry. I sent Tychicus to Ephesus… Erastus stayed in Corinth and I left Trophimus sick in Miletus. Do your best to get here before winter.

Paul's friends have regrouped since we last met them and some have scattered. Getting the whole family together for Christmas can be a similar problem. One person is going to the in-laws, another is on duty, another is going abroad, someone else is due for an operation, and so on. Everyone has their own life to live.

Paul is older now, approaching the end of his life, and again in prison. Everyone was away, most for perfectly good reasons. One was ill, one had delayed returning, several were on gospel business. But Paul was missing them. He asked Timothy to come with Mark quickly, before winter if possible.

Strong friendships can survive, and sometimes have to, without friends being able to see each other as much as they would like, and it is remarkable how we can 'pick up where we left off'. Without efficient mail, phone or modern media, it would have been much harder for Paul. How much more precious then was Luke who, alone of Paul's long-standing friends, was consistently there beside him.

■ PRAYER

Lord, help me to be realistic and understanding in what I expect in a friend. Amen

Job 42:7–10a (NIV, abridged)

Job's 'friends'

[The Lord] said to Eliphaz the Temanite, 'I am angry with you and your two friends, because you have not spoken the truth about me, as my servant Job has… My servant Job will pray for you, and I will accept his prayer and not deal with you according to your folly…' The Lord accepted Job's prayer. After Job had prayed for his friends, the Lord restored his fortunes.

Poor Job. His sufferings are legendary. During his earlier and later years, God blessed him with great prosperity but, in the middle, calamity after calamity caused him great misery. His suffering was made far worse by some inept friends, his so-called comforters. Were they well-meaning? Probably. But their lack of self-awareness and wisdom soon showed. As their 'counselling' progressed, they simply could not understand the impact of their unyielding words on someone experiencing Job's loss and grief. Some friends are hard work.

The 'patience of Job' is seen in his insistence that God is bigger and better than his friends' thinking allowed. Job showed considerable restraint with these friends and even found it in his heart to pray for them. The Lord heard, and restored Job's fortunes handsomely. Praying for others, particularly those friends we find hard to cope with, can release new blessing from God into our lives, and theirs.

■ **PRAYER**

Almighty God, even if I lose all I have and 'darkness is my closest friend', thank you that fellowship with you remains my greatest gift and the world's largest truth, in Christ Jesus. Amen

Proverbs 27:6, 9, 17 (NIV)

Bracing and reassuring

Wounds from a friend can be trusted, but an enemy multiplies kisses… Perfume and incense bring joy to the heart, and the pleasantness of a friend springs from their heartfelt advice… As iron sharpens iron, so one person sharpens another.

Picking soft fruit is a delicate business and I don't suppose that a robot could do it as well as human hands. When picking raspberries, for example, we have to adjust our touch each time so that our grip is firm enough to detach the fruit and yet gentle enough not to squash it.

Similarly, friendship has a firm side and a gentle side. 'Thank you for pulling me up,' said the great children's evangelist Hudson Pope, when a friend brought him some kind advice during an illness. A good friendship can be bracing and challenging, as well as cheering and reassuring. Even getting careful (and occasional!) criticism from a good friend can be a positive experience: we appreciate their understanding and insight and the fact that they care enough to challenge us.

The false kisses of an enemy are only too real in scripture, as in life. A true friend doesn't flatter, exploit or manipulate us, but speaks the truth in genuine love, respect and affection.

■ PRAYER

Lord Jesus Christ, you were full of grace and truth in all your dealings with people. May we model all our friendships on you. Redeemer, brother and friend, may we know you more clearly, love you more dearly and follow you more nearly all the days of our life. Amen

Giving for the future

16 September is the feast day of Saint Ninian. Now largely lost within the Anglican tradition, feast days are an annual celebration of a saint, usually marked by prayers and a relevant Bible reading.

Ninian lived during the fourth century and set up the first officially recognised community of God in Scotland, known as *Candida Casa* ('the white house'). In his book, *40 Days with the Celtic Saints* (BRF, 2017), David Cole says this was:

> ... a totally fresh expression of the Christian faith. Ninian stood out as someone different, someone holy, someone 'more'.

As society changes, there is a continuing need for the church to remain 'fresh' and stand out as something 'more'. This often means pioneering something new, and that's exactly what a church near Portsmouth did in 2004; they stepped out into the unknown and launched the first Messy Church. They had no idea that, 14 years later, it would be a worldwide movement, with almost 4,000 Messy Churches in over 25 countries.

BRF is the home of Messy Church, and through it we are helping families become followers of Jesus. For almost a century, we have been able to fund the growth, development and sustainability of programmes like Messy Church, thanks to the generosity of those who support us through gifts in wills.

If you share our vision for transforming lives through the Christian faith, would you consider leaving a gift in your will to BRF? It doesn't need to be huge to help us make a real difference.

For further information about making a gift to BRF in your will, please visit **brf.org.uk/lastingdifference**, contact Sophie Aldred on **+44 (0)1865 319700** or email **giving@brf.org.uk**.

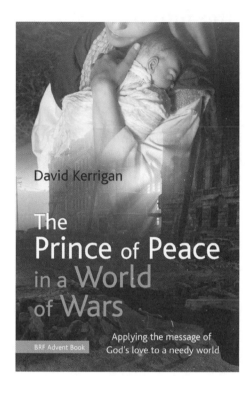

David Kerrigan sees the coming of Jesus at Christmas as central to the divine plan to bring peace to the world. Through daily reflection on biblical texts and mission stories, he locates God at the centre of our mission and encourages us to restore the peace, joy and hope that come from accompanying Jesus. But have we really understood what this peace might look like, especially in a world of wars and suffering?

The Prince of Peace in a World of Wars
Applying the message of God's love to a needy world
David Kerrigan
978 0 85746 570 2 £8.99
brfonline.org.uk

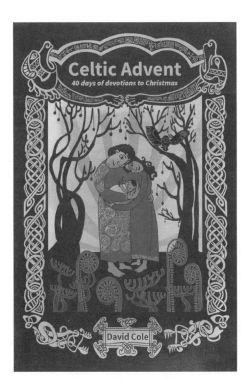

This inspirational book takes the reader through Advent to the celebration of Christmas through the eyes and beliefs of Celtic Christianity. Starting in November and reflecting on Jesus' coming at his birth as well as into our lives by the Holy Spirit and at the world's end, the author offers a unique approach to the season to help you gain a new sense of wonder in the birth of Jesus, the Saviour of the world.

Celtic Advent
40 days of devotions to Christmas
David Cole
978 0 85746 744 7 £8.99
brfonline.org.uk

To order

Online: **brfonline.org.uk**
Telephone: +44 (0)1865 319700
Mon–Fri 9.15–17.30
Post: complete this form and send to the address below

Delivery times within the UK are normally 15 working days. Prices are correct at the time of going to press but may change without prior notice.

Title	Issue*	Price	Qty	Total
The Prince of Peace in a World of Wars		£8.99		
Celtic Advent		£8.99		
Bible Reflections for Older People (single copy)	Jan/May* 19	£4.99		

delete as appropriate

POSTAGE AND PACKING CHARGES			
Order value	UK	Europe	Rest of world
Under £7.00	£2.00	£5.00	£7.00
£7.00–£29.99	£3.00	£9.00	£15.00
£30.00 and over	FREE	£9.00 + 15% of order value	£15.00 + 20% of order value

Total value of books	
Postage and packing	
Total for this order	

Please complete in BLOCK CAPITALS

Title .... First name/initials .... Surname ....

Address ....

.... Postcode ....

Acc. No. .... Telephone ....

Email ....

Method of payment

❏ Cheque (made payable to BRF)   ❏ MasterCard / Visa

Card no. ☐☐☐☐ ☐☐☐☐ ☐☐☐☐ ☐☐☐☐

Valid from M M Y Y   Expires M M Y Y   Security code* ☐☐☐

Last 3 digits on the reverse of the card

Signature* .... Date .... / .... / ....

*ESSENTIAL IN ORDER TO PROCESS YOUR ORDER

Please return this form to:
BRF, 15 The Chambers, Vineyard, Abingdon OX14 3FE | enquiries@brf.org.uk
To read our terms and conditions, please visit **brfonline.org.uk/terms**.

The Bible Reading Fellowship (BRF) is a Registered Charity (233280)

BIBLE REFLECTIONS FOR OLDER PEOPLE GROUP SUBSCRIPTION FORM

> All our Bible reading notes can be ordered online
> by visiting **biblereadingnotes.org.uk/subscriptions**

The group subscription rate for *Bible Reflections for Older People* will be £14.97 per person until April 2019.

☐ I would like to take out a group subscription for .... (*quantity*) copies.

☐ Please start my order with the January 2019 / May 2019 / September 2019* issue. I would like to pay annually/receive an invoice with each edition of the notes.* (*delete as appropriate*)

Please do not send any money with your order. Send your order to BRF and we will send you an invoice. The group subscription year is from 1 May to 30 April. If you start subscribing in the middle of a subscription year we will invoice you for the remaining number of issues left in that year.

Name and address of the person organising the group subscription:

Title .... First name/initials .... Surname ....

Address ....

.... Postcode ....

Telephone .... Email ....

Church ....

Name of minister ....

Name and address of the person paying the invoice if the invoice needs to be sent directly to them:

Title .... First name/initials .... Surname ....

Address ....

.... Postcode ....

Telephone .... Email ....

Please return this form to:
BRF, 15 The Chambers, Vineyard, Abingdon OX14 3FE | enquiries@brf.org.uk
To read our terms and conditions, please visit brfonline.org.uk/terms.

BROP0318   The Bible Reading Fellowship is a Registered Charity (233280)

BIBLE REFLECTIONS FOR OLDER PEOPLE INDIVIDUAL/GIFT SUBSCRIPTION FORM

To order online, please visit **biblereadingnotes.org.uk/subscriptions**

☐ I would like to take out a subscription (*complete your name and address details only once*)

☐ I would like to give a gift subscription (*please provide both names and addresses*)

Title .... First name/initials .... Surname ....

Address ....

.... Postcode ....

Telephone .... Email ....

Gift subscription name ....

Gift subscription address ....

.... Postcode ....

Gift message (*20 words max. or include your own gift card*):

....

....

Please send **Bible Reflections for Older People** beginning with the January 2019 / May 2019 / September 2019* issue (**delete as appropriate*):

(*please tick box*)	UK	Europe	Rest of world
Bible Reflections for Older People	☐ £18.75	☐ £26.70	☐ £30.75

Total enclosed £ .... (*cheques should be made payable to 'BRF'*)

Please charge my MasterCard / Visa ☐ Debit card ☐ with £ ....

Card no. ☐☐☐☐ ☐☐☐☐ ☐☐☐☐ ☐☐☐☐

Valid from M M Y Y   Expires M M Y Y   Security code* ☐☐☐

Last 3 digits on the reverse of the card

Signature* .... Date ..../......../........

*ESSENTIAL IN ORDER TO PROCESS YOUR ORDER

Please return this form to:
BRF, 15 The Chambers, Vineyard, Abingdon OX14 3FE | enquiries@brf.org.uk
To read our terms and conditions, please visit brfonline.org.uk/terms.

BROP0318   The Bible Reading Fellowship is a Registered Charity (233280)